[BERNARD MANDEVILLE]

THE
MISCHIEFS

THAT OUGHT

Justly to be Apprehended

FROM A

Whig-Government.

(1714)

Introduction by

H. T. DICKINSON

WILDSIDE PRESS

INTRODUCTION

In recent years there has been a major revival of interest in the work and influence of Bernard Mandeville. Much of this interest has, quite naturally, concentrated on his most famous work, *The Fable of the Bees,* and on his influence on, and relationship to, the ethics, economic thought, and literature of the eighteenth century.[1] Little attempt has been made to analyze his political thought or to establish his attitude towards contemporary politics.[2] This neglect is understandable though not entirely justified. Very little is known about Mandeville's personal life and activities. There is not much evidence in his authenticated works to link him directly to contemporary politics. Moreover, the one overtly political pamphlet which has been attributed to him, *The Mischiefs that ought Justly to be Apprehended from a Whig-Government* (London, 1714), has been ignored because it cannot be identified as Mandeville's work with absolute certainty. If, however, it can be shown that there is very strong evidence for attributing *The Mischiefs* to Mandeville, then a new political dimension to his work can be explored more thoroughly than ever before. This introduction is an attempt to present the evidence, both external and internal, which can be marshalled to support the claim that Mandeville was indeed the author of *The Mischiefs.* If this is in fact the case, then Mandeville must be regarded as a thoroughgoing, though moderate, Whig, who felt the need to join in the campaign to safeguard the Hanoverian succession after the death of Queen Anne in 1714.

It has been suggested that Mandeville could not have written *The Mischiefs* because he never showed much interest in contemporary politics.[3] The evidence presented below will show that this was not in fact the case, though, of course, it can be maintained that Mandeville was never a political bigot nor a committed partisan in the Whig-Tory disputes of the early eighteenth century. This would indeed have been foreign to his ironic, even cynical, view of human nature, his realistic appreciation of human weakness, and his opposition to intolerant or extremist views. Moreover, a number of specific quotations can be taken from his published works to illustrate his general reluctance to follow a party line. In his *Free Thoughts on Religion, the Church, and National Happiness*, Mandeville declared: "I despise the very Thoughts of a Party-Man, and desire to touch no Man's Sore, but in order to heal it."[4] Even more categorical is the statement by Cleomenes, in *An Enquiry into the Origin of Honour and the Usefulness of Christianity in War*, that he will have nothing to do with Whigs or Tories.[5] In the second volume of *The Fable of the Bees*, Cleomenes warns Horatio that he will avoid entering into party disputes with him[6] and at the end of *Free Thoughts on Religion, the Church and National Happiness*, Mandeville confesses that he wished he could cure men of the folly of enlisting in parties.[7] Certainly Mandeville himself never hired his pen to any party, and, in *A Letter to Dion*, he expressed his contempt for such party hacks in unmistakable terms.[8]

Such evidence only shows that Mandeville was critical of political extremism and party-hacks. It does not mean that he could not have held and expressed the moderate Whig views found in *The Mischiefs*. There were many Whigs who did not relish the party battle and who hoped to bind up the wounds of the nation. They would have sympathized with the declaration made by Mandeville in *The Female Tatler*:

> We are of that Party that far from siding with any, instead of corroding Arguments to uphold the one against the other, studies how to prevent the Misunderstandings, and allay the Anmosities of all, that without wishing ill, much less destroying, either Party would extirpate the Names of both, and Heal up the Wounds of our unhappy Divisions, with that admirable *panacea* of Concord and Unanimity.[9]

Nevertheless, while Mandeville might not have been an active partisan, there can be no doubt that his political sympathies lay with the Whigs. From what is known of his life, and from the many clues that can be gleaned from his various published works, it is clear that Mandeville agreed with all the major points made by the author of *The Mischiefs*.

Bernard Mandeville was a Dutchman, born in Rotterdam in 1670, who came to England in the 1690s, shortly after the Glorious Revolution. It is highly likely that, as a Dutchman, Mandeville would have sympathized with the Whigs who had done so much to put Dutch William on the throne and who were staunch supporters of the Dutch alliance. Moreover, no Dutchman would have found a welcome in the Tory camp for the Tories were notorious for their hostility to the Dutch.[10] Of Mandeville's few known acquaintances only one, Thomas Parker, later Earl of Macclesfield, was a politician, but he was a thorough-going Whig. Parker was the most able Whig manager in the celebrated impeachment in 1710 of the high-flying Tory, Dr. Henry Sacheverell,[11] and he was advanced to the posts of Lord Chief Justice and Lord Chancellor by Whig patronage and influence.

An examination of Mandeville's own political views, expressed in many of his authenticated works, shows that they are in harmony with the main points made in *The Mischiefs*. In the tense political atmosphere between the death of Queen Anne and the outbreak of the Jacobite rebellion of 1715 this pamphlet was one of the more moderate defences of the Hanoverian succession.[12] *The Mischiefs* upholds, without rancor, the main principles in favor of a limited monarchy and in opposition to the theories of divine right, non-resistance, and passive obedience which would sustain an absolute monarchy. It is committed to the Protestant succession in the House of Hanover and opposes a Jacobite restoration. It condemns the high-Church extremists and supports the religious toleration granted to Protestant Dissenters. It criticizes the Tories for their lukewarm support for the recently-concluded war against Louis XIV and for their decision to desert the allies and sign a separate peace treaty with France. Most significantly of all, it makes a special point of arguing that the nation has nothing to fear from a foreign king or from other foreigners who might come into the country. None of these views can be regarded as being in conflict with the declared opinions of Mandeville and, indeed, every one of them can be supported by arguments taken from his authenticated works.

There can be no doubt that Mandeville rejected the Tory political theories of divine right, non-resistance, and passive obedience, and supported the Revolution of 1688 and the constitutional ideals of a limited monarchy and a mixed government. In chapter eleven of *Free Thoughts on Religion, the Church and National Happiness*, Mandeville expressed his political and constitutional views at some length. While admitting that there could be no perfect form of government and that each form had its peculiar disadvantages, he expressed his preference for the mixed government of Britain. This mixed government combined monarchy, aristocracy and democracy, in the form of King, Lords and Commons, and sought to secure the benefits of each while avoiding the inconveniences normally associated with each of them in its pure form. Such a constitution would protect the prerogatives of the crown and safeguard the liberties of the subject. Like all sound Whigs, however, Mandeville was more concerned about the threat which an unrestrained monarch might pose to the rights of the people. It was therefore important to stress that: "The Rights and Privileges of Parliament, and the Liberty of the People are as Sacred Branches of the Constitution as any thing the King can claim."[13] While taking care not to encourage the resistance of the people to their lawful sovereign, Mandeville believed that such resistance was less heinous an offence than the exercise of arbitrary power.[14] The civil war of the seventeenth century, Mandeville maintains, was caused by Charles I and his supporters rejecting this mixed form of government in favor of an absolute monarchy based on the theory of the divine right of kings.[15] Only by rejecting such a theory, and the associated notions of non-resistance, passive obedience, and indefeasible hereditary succession, were the people able to protect their political liberties in 1688.[16] To secure a mixed government and a limited monarchy, it was necessary for the nation to abandon James II and the Pretender, and to accept William III, the defender of both English and European liberties.[17] This praise for William III and his policies, particularly the defence of Europe against the ambitions of Louis XIV of France, was also the burden of another work, *The Pamphleteers: A Satyr* (London, 1703), which has sometimes been attributed to Mandeville.[18]

There can be even less doubt about the claim that Mandeville shared the same religious views as the author of *The*

Mischiefs. Throughout his works Mandeville criticized the pretensions of the clergy, accused them of inciting disputes and interfering in political affairs, and advocated a policy of religious toleration among those Protestants who disagreed only in minor questions of ceremony and organization. In his *Free Thoughts on Religion, the Church and National Happiness,* and, to a lesser extent, in *An Enquiry into the Origin of Honour and the Usefulness of Christianity in War,* Mandeville savagely attacked the worldly ambitions, the hypocrisy, and the intolerance of the Roman Catholic Church in particular, but he did not spare the various Protestant sects. He made a strong plea for men to put an end to the unnecessary and destructive disputes between the clergy of the Church of England and the Dissenters.[19] While advocating a policy of toleration for the different Protestant sects, however, Mandeville did not wish to extend such a policy to Roman Catholics because they could not be trusted to support the existing political settlement.[20]

In his contributions to *The Female Tatler,* written in 1709-1710, Mandeville applied himself more specifically to the impact on contemporary politics of the religious disputes waged by intolerant divines. He showed himself particularly concerned with the political and religious tension created by the notorious sermon of Dr. Henry Sacheverell. In St. Paul's, on 5 November 1709, the anniversary of William III's landing at Torbay in 1688, Sacheverell had preached a sermon on "The Perils of False Brethren," which attacked not only the Whig ministers then in office, but the Toleration Act and the political principles that underlay the Revolution. Mandeville joined most other Whigs in condemning both the tone and the arguments of this inflammatory sermon. In *The Female Tatler,* published 14-16 November 1709, Mandeville described a dream in which Emilia met a clergyman, clearly from England, who lamented the religious disputes which were destroying the stability and happiness of his native land.[21] A month after Sacheverell's sermon, on 5 December 1709, Mandeville inserted this satirical advertizement in *The Female Tatler:*

There is now in the press and will be speedily publish'd, The Case of *Passive Obedience,* truly stated in a *Sermon* preached in the Chief *Mosque* of *Constantinople* in the *Christian* Time, call'd St. *Sophia;* shewing, that the Deposition of *Mahomet* in the Year 88. was contrary to the Rules of the *Alcoran.* By *Sache-ali-Verello,* a Seditious Priest, that having no other Merits, would fain have dy'd a Martyr for the cause, but was preserved by the Lenity of the Successors. Translated by a *Non Juror* [italics reversed].[22]

Mandeville also shared the Whig conviction that everything possible must be done to curb the over-mighty power of Louis XIV. In *The Virgin Unmask'd,* the dialogues between Lucinda and Antonia are full of references to the need for the European powers to unite in opposition to the King of France. Of the two, Antonia is much more prejudiced against Louis XIV and more convinced of the suffering he had inflicted on Europe. Lucinda is prepared to acknowledge that Louis XIV had done much to promote arts and sciences, but this only serves to make her condemnation of him more effective:

Can any one love Liberty, and not abhor that harden'd Monster of Ambition? To whom the greatest Losses and Calamities of His friends, are not unwelcome, if they can but advance his Glory. That arbitrary Fiend, that knowing himself to be the Cause of War and Famine, beholds the Miseries of his own People with less Concern than you can see a Play; the Bane of Mankind, that can draw whole Schemes of the Destruction and Devastation of florishing Cities and plentiful Countries, with the same Tranquility as I can play a Game at Chess.[23]

Mandeville had no illusions about the glory of war and frequently ridiculed men who risked their lives in the pursuit of honour and fame,[24] but he entertained no doubts about the need to fight France. In *The Female Tatler,* Mandeville, using the "Oxford Student" to voice his own ethical views, criticizes the vanity of soldiers, but he is prepared to admit the justice of the war against Louis XIV.[25] On several other occasions Mandeville praised Marlborough and the troops who took the field against the French.[26] He believed that the cost of the war had to be borne by all the allies. Unlike the Tories, who complained about the heavy land tax of four shillings in the pound that was needed to pay for the war, he believed that the Dutch were bearing a greater proportion of the financial burden when they paid their hundred penny tax.[27]

This defense of the Dutch, made only by Whigs in 1709, leads us naturally to the last and perhaps strongest, external clue linking Mandeville to *The Mischiefs*. The author of this pamphlet is at pains to combat the xenophobia of the Tories and to argue that a foreign king was no threat to any British interest. This endeavor would certainly have commended itself to Mandeville. He was naturally sympathetic to the Dutch and he admired both their achievements in general and William III's in particular.[28] Moreover, he deliberately sought to reconcile those who feared the way George I favored servants he had brought over with him from Hanover to this disagreeable but temporary situation:

Most of our Fore fathers were once Strangers, but the first Children, they begot here, were *English*. When Courtiers, that are Foreigners enrich themselves with our Money, their Heirs spend it among us, and the Sons often with the same Application, that the Fathers scrap'd it together.[29]

Thus, an examination of Mandeville's known political views shows that they are in accord with those of the author of *The Mischiefs*. Such external evidence, however, can only suggest that Mandeville might have written this pamphlet. It requires internal evidence to link Mandeville directly to *The Mischiefs*. The internal evidence available is not entirely conclusive, but there are a number of clues which, added together, build a strong case for maintaining that Mandeville was indeed the author of this political tract.[30] Copies of *The Mischiefs* have been traced to three libraries: the British Museum, the Bodleian Library and the William Andrews Clark Memorial Library. All three libraries attribute the pamphlet to Mandeville. Moreover, on the copy at the Clark Library and on one of the copies at the

Bodleian,[31] the name of Mandeville has long ago been added to the title page.

The Mischiefs also shares some stylistic similarities with the known works of Mandeville. It is in the form of a dialogue[32] and it is typically Mandevillian in its use of irony, wit, logic, and parable. In two cases there are close parallels of argument, even of phrasing. In the Free Thoughts on Religion, the Church and National Happiness (1729 ed., p. 325) and in The Mischiefs (p. 17) there is the same defense of religious toleration based on the argument that the Church of England is a dissenting church in Scotland just as the Presbyterian church is a dissenting body in England. Moreover, the same examples are cited of a mob pulling down a meeting house in England and a mob abusing the Book of Common Prayer in Scotland. In the second case, the argument in the Free Thoughts (1729 ed., pp. 48-50) that the Protestants' hatred of the crucifix is as absurd as the Catholics' worship of it is paralleled in both reasoning and phraseology by a passage in The Mischiefs (pp. 30-31).

Probably the strongest single piece of internal evidence linking Mandeville to the authorship of The Mischiefs is the woodcut decoration used in this pamphlet. The Mischiefs has two woodcut ornaments—one of a vase, on the title-page, and the other of a lion, on page three, heading the text. Both of these woodcuts are found in the 1714 edition of The Fable of the Bees, published by Roberts, who produced The Mischiefs, but also in three editions of the Free Thoughts, each produced by a different publisher.[33] These ornaments could have been passed from one publisher to another without any reference to Mandeville, but, since these woodcuts have not been found in any other works except those of Mandeville, it appears more likely that Mandeville owned them and allowed them to be used only in his own works.[34] It should come as no surprize to any student of Mandeville if the woodcut of the lion, which is reproduced no fewer than three times in the 1720 edition of the Free Thoughts, belonged to Mandeville rather than to his publisher or printer. He was certainly fascinated by lions. In volume two of The Fable of the Bees, Cleomenes declares:

there is nothing I admire more than a Lion . . . . What I admire, is his Fabrick, his Structure, and his Rage, so justly proportion'd to one another. There are Order, Symmetry, and superlative Wisdom to be observ'd in all the Works of Nature; but she has not a Machine, of which every Part more visibly answers the End, for which the whole was form'd. . . . there is real Majesty stamp'd on every single Lion, at the sight of which, the stoutest Animals submit and tremble.[35]

Edinburgh University

NOTES TO THE INTRODUCTION

1. Any study of Mandeville's works and influence must begin with F. B. Kaye's edition of *The Fable of the Bees* (2 vols., Oxford: Clarendon Press 1924) and the same author's paper "The Influence of Bernard Mandeville," in *Studies in Philology*, XIX, (1922), 83-108. Recent important articles, none of which bear directly on Mandeville's views on contemporary politics, include J. C. Maxwell, "Ethics and Politics in Mandeville," *Philosophy*, XXVI, (1951), 242-52; Philip Harth, "The Satiric Purpose of the Fable of the Bees," *Eighteenth-Century Studies*, II, (1962), 321-40; Nathan Rosenberg, "Mandeville and Laissez-Faire," *Journal of the History of Ideas*, XXIV, (1963), 183-96; Thomas R. Edwards, "Mandeville's Moral Prose," *ELH*, XXXI, (1964), 195-212; Martin Price, *To the Palace of Wisdom* (Garden City, N.Y.: Doubleday, 1964), pp. 105-08; F. A. Hayek, "Dr. Bernard Mandeville," *Proceedings of the British Academy*, LII, (1966), 125-41; M. J. Scott-Taggart, "Mandeville: Cynic or Fool?," *Philosophical Quarterly*, XVI, (1966), 221-32; and John Colman, "Bernard Mandeville and the Reality of Virtue," *Philosophy*, XLVII, (1972), 125-39.

2. Of the works listed in the previous footnote, only Rosenberg and, to a lesser extent, Maxwell have discussed Mandeville's political thought. Only Isaac Kramnick, in *Bolingbroke and His Circle* (Cambridge, Mass: Harvard Univ. Press, 1968), pp. 201-4, has made an attempt to link Mandeville directly to the contemporary political scene.

3. This was one of the main arguments put forward by Paul Sakmann in *Bernard Mandeville und die Bienenfabel-Controversie* (Freiburg, 1897), p. 38. Sakmann's conclusion was rejected by F. B. Kaye in "The Writings of Bernard Mandeville: A Bibliographical Survey," *Journal of English and Germanic Philology*, XX, (1921), 448-50 and in his introduction to *The Fable of the Bees*, vol. I, p. xxxi, note 5. No one has since challenged Kay's verdict.

4. *Free Thoughts* (1723 ed.), p. 152.

5. *Origin of Honour*, p. 139.

6. Vol. II, p. 42.

7. *Free Thoughts* (1723 ed.), pp. 362-63.

8. *A Letter to Dion* (1732 ed.), p. 8; (and ARS Publication Number 41).

9. *The Female Tatler*, no. 100 (wrongly printed as no. 97), 22 Feb. 1710.

10. See my paper, "The Tory Party's Attitude to Foreigners," *Bulletin of the Institute of Historical Research*, XL, (1967), 153-65.

11. See Geoffrey Holmes, *The Trial of Doctor Sacheverell* (London: Eyre Methuen, 1973), pp. 149-55.

12. *The Mischiefs* never descends to bitter invective nor to personal abuse. It makes no attack on any of the late Tory ministers, which was a common line of criticism by many other pamphleteers in 1714, and offers nothing in praise of the Whig leaders. Note the comment on p. 39: "Let the King employ whom he pleases as long as the welfare of the Nation is observ'd, I shall never trouble my head who is In or Out, and a Prince that was Just whilst he rul'd as he pleas'd, will never govern the worse when he has good Laws to guide him."

13. *Free Thoughts* (1723 ed.), p. 305. Compare this quotation with the statement in *The Mischiefs*, p. 29: "the People have their Privileges, and all the Blessings they enjoy as much from God as the King his Prerogative."

14. *An Enquiry into the Origin of Honour and the Usefulness of Christianity in War*, pp. 170-71. Cf. "There is Nothing more universal than the Love of Liberty." *Ibid.*, p. 177.

15. *Free Thoughts* (1723 ed.), pp. 298-99 and *Origin of Honour*, pp. 163-65. Compare these observations with *The Mischiefs*, pp. 21-23.

16. *Free Thoughts* (1723 ed.), pp. 309-15. See also the advertisement Mandeville printed in *The Female Tatler*, no. 75 (26 Dec. 1709), for the sale of "A Scaffold upon *Tower Hill*, little the worse for wearing, to be disposed of at Reasonable Rates, to any Person who shall have so little Religion, Sense or good Manners, either in Church or Coffee House, to sow Sedition, and repine at our present most glorious Constitution" [italics reversed]. This was aimed at Dr. Henry Sacheverell, whose sermon on 5 November 1709 had attacked the principles of the Glorious Revolution.

17. *Free Thoughts* (1723 ed.), pp. 321-28. See also the fears of a Jacobite restoration expressed on pp. 352-54.

18. This pamphlet, in verse form, is attributed to Mandeville by the British Museum and the Newberry Library. It is a thorough-going defence of William III and his Whig ministers against the supporters of Popery and arbitrary government. It expresses particular annoyance at the way William III was so abused after his death; a view that Mandeville probably shared.

19. *Free Thoughts* (1723 ed.), p. 57.

20. *Ibid.*, pp. 241-42.

21. *The Female Tatler*, no. 57.

22. *Ibid.*, no. 66.

23. *The Virgin Unmask'd: Or, Female Dialogues betwixt an elderly Maiden Lady, and her Niece* (1709), p. 181.

24. *The Fable of the Bees*, ed. F. B. Kaye, I, 63; *The Female Tatler*, no. 84, 16 Jan. 1709/10; *Origin of Honour*, esp. the 3rd dialogue.

25. *The Female Tatler*, no. 84, 16 Jan. 1709/10.

26. *The Fable of the Bees*, ed. F. B. Kaye, II, 337-39; *Origin of Honour*, p. 139; *The Virgin Unmask'd*, pp. 133, 148, 151.

27. *The Virgin Unmask'd*, pp. 138-39.

28. *Free Thoughts* (1723 ed.), pp. 327-28; *The Fable of the Bees*, ed. F. B. Kaye, I, 185-91; and *The Pamphleteers: A Satyr* (London, 1703).

29. *Free Thoughts* (1723 ed.), p. 351.

30. Most of these were made by F. B. Kaye in "The Writings of Bernard Mandeville: A Bibliographical Survey," *Journal of English and Germanic Philology*, **XX**, (1921), 448-50.

31. Pamphlet GP399(5).

32. Mandeville used the dialogue form in *The Fable of the Bees*, vol. II; *The Female Tatler*; *Origin of Honour*; *The Virgin Unmask'd*; and *A Treatise of the Hypochondriak and Hysterick Passions*. In *The Female Tatler*, no. 60, one of the disputants is called "Lovetruth," which is very similar to the "Loveright" used in *The Mischiefs*.

33. The 1720 edition was published by Roberts and Jauncy, the 1721 edition by Warner, and the 1723 edition by Brotherton.

34. It is certainly additional, although not conclusive, evidence that other wood-cut ornaments keep reappearing in the works of Mandeville. For example, the woodcut on p. i of the Preface and p. 1 of the text of *An Enquiry into the Causes of the Frequent Executions at Tyburn* (published by Roberts), also appears on pp. 1 and 443 of the 1724 edition of *The Fable of the Bees* and p. i of the Preface and p. 27 of the 1728 edition of *The Fable* (both published by Tonson); and the woodcut on the title-page of *A Letter to Dion* (published by Roberts) is reproduced on p. xi of *Origin of Honour* (published by Brotherton).

35. *The Fable of the Bees*, ed. F. B. Kaye, II, 233. See the continuation of Cleomenes' remarks on p. 234 and also *ibid.*, I, 176-81.

A NOTE ON THE TEXT

I have been able to trace only five copies of *The Mischiefs*. The Bodleian possesses no fewer than three of these. The others are in the British Museum and the William Andrews Clark Memorial Library.

The Mischiefs was published late in 1714. The text suggests that it was after George I's arrival in England, on 18 September, and possibly after his coronation, on 20 October 1714. One copy in the Bodleian, listed as GP1147(14), has the date "17 Novemb." written on the title-page in a very old hand. F. B. Kaye noted that a second edition of *The Mischiefs* was advertised in the *Post Man* for 4-7 December 1714, which suggests that the first edition must have sold well. All the extant copies are from the same, presumably the first, edition.

BIBLIOGRAPHICAL NOTE

The facsimile of *The Mischiefs* (1714) is reproduced by permission from the unbound copy
(Pam. Coll.) in the William Andrews Clark
Memorial Library. The total type-page (p. 9)
measures 155 x 74 mm.

THE

MISCHIEFS

THAT OUGHT

Juftly to be Apprehended

FROM A

Whig-Government.

Bernard Mandeville
M. D.

L O N D O N:

nted for I. ROBERTS, near the *Oxford-Arms*
in *Warwick-Lane,* 1714.

(*Price Six-Pence.*)

B. Mandeville.

A DIALOGUE

BETWEEN

Tantivy and *Loveright.*

Tant. YOU are welcome to *Town*, Loveright.

Love. I thank you.

Tant. *I have not seen you this Reign: Now sure you are pleas'd, the Party carries it swimingly.*

Loveright. Without doubt am I pleas'd, and so I hope is every true *Briton*, to see his Country, by so unexpected a turn of Providence, snatch'd from the Jaws of Popery and Perdition.

Tant. *You Whigs are admirably qualify'd for Poetry and the Stage ; you first forge* Harpies, Sphinxes, Dragons, *and* Chimeras, *that*

never were in Nature, and then to put them off
for Reallities upon the People, you start and pre-
tend to be frightned at the Monsters of your own
Invention.

Lov. But do you *Tories* think that ftale way
of bantering People out of their Senfes and
denying your Defigns till the Moment they
are executed, will always impofe upon the
World ? Did you not talk much after the
fame Rate, when, in the late Reign, from
fome Alterations at Court, and other bad
Prefages, Men apprehended that the Em-
peror's Intereft was going to be abandon'd,
all our Allies left in the Lurch, and a
Peace with *France* refolv'd upon at any
Rate ? How groundlefs and unreafonable
were the Fears of the *Whigs* then ! What
Affurances had we from the Throne to the
contrary ? And yet thefe Apprehenfions
prov'd juft, a feparate and inglorious Peace
is patch'd up with *France*, the Houfe of
Bourbon left in poffeffion of *Spain* and the
Weft Indies, that of *Auftria* forfaken, and
the reft of our Allies either bully'd into
the fame difadvantageous Peace, or bid to
fhift for themfelves : But with all my
Heart, the Fears of the Pretender were
only a Trick of the *Whigs* to render the
Miniftry odious to the People ; the lifting
of Men into his Service, the difarming of
Proteftants, and countenancing of Papifts
in *Ireland*, the bare-fac'd Impudence. and
treafonable Practices of the Jacobites in
Scotland and the defign of new modelling
and changing all the Officers of the Army,
with

with the reſt of the Proceedings throughout the three Kingdoms had no manner of
Tendency towards the bringing in of the
Pretender ; tho' the *French* openly talk'd of
it as an Enterprize ſo well concerted, that
it could not miſcarry ; and at *Paris* People
were laugh'd at if they were ſo filly as to
doubt of it. If all theſe were Signs of no
ſignification, it ſhall never coſt me a Moment's Quiet ; if our Fears about the Pretender were groundleſs before, I'm glad
we are cured of them now : But what's
the Matter the High-flyers look all ſo down
in the Mouth; the *Tories*, you know, were always for the *Hanover* Succeſſion ; the King
is ſafely arrived, and ſettled on his Throne
in a ſurprizing Tranquility, the *French* King
looks on, and all our Allies that had been
diſguſted drop their Reſentments, and joyn
with us in the common Joy. When Men's
Wiſhes are compleat, they don't uſe to be
out of Humour.

Tant. *When the King, who is but a Stranger
among us yet, once comes to know what the
Whigs are, I dare ſay you won't be ſo Cock-a-
hoop ?*

Love. How great a Stranger to our Affairs you take King *George* to be, I don't
know, but I am much miſtaken if ſome People find him not better inform'd of all the
Tranſactions of the late Miniſtry than
they could have either wiſh'd or imagin'd ;
but pray what could you tell him of the
Whigs that he is ignorant of ?

Tant.

Tant. That they are inveterate Enemies to Monarchy, and that all Kings and Queens, sooner or later, repented that they employ'd any.

Love. If, instead of Monarchy, you had said Tyranny, and prefix'd the Word Arbitrary to Kings and Queens, I would not have deny'd the Charge; for a *Whig* is one that stands up for Liberty and Property and the Welfare of the Nation, that is Obedient and Submissive to his Sovereign, as long as he rules by Law, and endeavours to promote the Good of his Subjects, but thinks it lawful whenever the King, or his Favourites, invade the Constitution, and break in upon the Privileges of the People, to resist both him and his Ministers. This the King knows, and a just Prince who thinks his Coronation Oath as binding upon himself, as that of Allegiance is upon his Subjects, has no occasion for the Doctrine of *Non-Resistance.* *Whigs* may make Disturbances when Princes turn Tyrants, but when a King is of the same Principles, and there is no clashing between Privileges and Prerogative, what Mischief can you apprehend from such a *Whig-Government ?*

Tant. *The extirpation of* Episcopacy, *without which* Monarchy *in* England *cannot subsist long ; for this Reason the* Whigs *love no Kings but Strangers, who having no right of Inheritance to rely on, they hope will in Gratitude to their Electors, part with what Branch of the Prerogative the* Whigs *shall want to accomplish their old design of sapping the Regal Power, till,*

by

by sharing it among them, they can once more make it dwindle into a Commonwealth.

Love. This is the old Story, the Church is in Danger, tho no Body can tell why or where, and whenever a King grasps not at Arbitrary Power, the High-flyers are a-fraid *Monarchy* is a going to be lost ; how can they ever pretend to laugh at the Fears of others that can entertain such silly ones of their own ? In King *William's* time they pretended to be afraid that after his De-cease we should have no more Kings or Queens, and on all occasions insinuated, as if that Prince endeavour'd to leave *England* a Commonwealth ; but if those Jealousies were groundless, as Experience has taught us, when we had a King, who, during his whole Reign, was likely to dye without Issue, and when his Queen and the Duke of *Gloucester* were dead, could leave no Heir or Successor to the Crown, whom he had reason greatly to care for, how ridi-culous must they be in the Reign of a Prince, who, besides Daughters, has so dutiful a Son, in whose numerous Off-spring he has so glorious a Prospect of wor-thy Successors that are dear to him ?

Tant. *We never had a Native of* England, *for whose Memory the* Whigs *have such a Vene-ration as they have for that of* King William, *by whose means they have got another Foreigner to be our King.*

Love. That *D——* Legacy I find sticks strangely in your Stomach.

Tant. *Nay,*

Tant. Nay, I own you have other Reasons besides to remember your Dutch *King: The Trienniel Parliaments, and other Acts that lessen'd the Regal Authority, were of his making ; our Monarchs now are no more than the Kings of* Sparta, *that have a perpetual Assembly of* Ephori *to tutor and contradict them. The* Whigs *are ever fond of Princes that suffer them to diminish the Prerogative, which by their means is already so clip'd and curtail'd, the Crown is hardly worth wearing, and a King of* Great Britain *is not much more than a* Doge *of* Venice.

Love. If Raving, Falfities and Contradictions were convincing Arguments, there would be no difputing with the *Tories*. What Parity pray is there between a King of *Great Britain* and a Doge of *Venice* as to Power? I would not tire you with the many Branches of the King's Prerogative, which a Doge of *Venice* is wholly deftitute of ; but fhall only name a few, and afterwards give you leave to examine into the Juftice of your Comparifon your felf. The King has the Power to difpofe of the Publick Revenue, and name all Officers Ecclefiaftical and Civil, that are of Truft or Profit in the Kingdom: He has an Abfolute Command over the whole Militia both by Sea and Land, and all the Nation together cannot make one Law without his Confent. Whoever confiders the weight of thefe Articles, will find that the Sovereign's Power is exceffive great, and muft be dreadful in the Hands of bad Princes ; our Kings then being invefted with fo vaft

an

an Authority, have we not Reason to wish
for and be fond of Monarchs that are of
moderate Principles, and will not abuse it?
Whenever our Sovereigns have talk'd much
of their Prerogative, and threaten'd us
with their firm Resolutions they had not
to recede an Inch from it, it has always
been with a design of exerting it to the
dislike of the People. Hence arose that
universal Joy in the Hearts of all true
Britons when they saw their present Sovereign, instead of Contending for what
might be due to himself, bend his first
Cares to secure the Property of his Subjects.
Where Justice and Wisdom reign, and no
other Interest but that of the whole Nation prevails, 'tis no great Matter whether
the Prince himself be a Native or a Foreigner, and that the High-flyers in speaking of the King so often repeat the Word
Stranger, is only because they know that
among ignorant and ill bred People, 'tis an
invidious Name : They vent their Spleen
by it with impunity, and therefore had
King *George* been bred and born in *China*,
and his Family never been related to any
Christian Prince in *Europe*, they could lay
no greater stress upon his being a Stranger
than some of them do. His Majesty's
Grandmother, the Queen of *Bohemia*, was
an *English* Woman, who, in all probability,
brought up her Children her own way :
The Princess her Daughter, who was the
Mother of our present Sovereign has been
next Heir to the Crown for almost Four-
teen Years, and her self being of a great

Age

Age, and our late Queen the greateſt part of her Reign in an ill State of Health, his Majeſty has had a Proſpeƈt a great many Years that he was to fill the *Britiſh* Throne; beſides that, ever ſince the Aƈt of Succeſſion the Court of *Hanover* has never been without *Engliſh* Men. Can any Body think that a wiſe Prince, who has had ſo much time, and ſo many Opportunities over and over to be inform'd even of the leaſt Trifles relating to *Great Britain*, ſhould not have thoroughly examin'd into the Affairs of three Kingdoms of ſo near, and ſo great a Concern to him, or that he ſhould not have ſtudy'd the Temper and Genius of a Nation, which, in all Human Probability, it would be his Right one Day to govern; and therefore can it be imagined but that the King, long before now, has been well verſed in every thing relating to our Cuſtoms, Manner and Conſtitution, that can any ways be worthy the Notice of a Prince? Then why is he a Stranger?

Tant. *That's very plain; becauſe this is* Great Britain, *and the King was born in* Germany. *All Nations reckon it a Happineſs to be rul'd by Princes that are born among them, and every Body knows that Men generally have a more Natural Affeƈtion for the Places of their Birth, than they can have for any other.*

Love. 'Tis very wrong for private Men to meaſure the Sentiments of Princes by their own: Thoſe that move in higher Spheres, have but ſeldom ſuch narrow Views. But to argue your own way; there is not one Quality that makes us

love

love things more than their being our
own; all People Naturally love their
Poſſeſſions. Suppoſe a very fine Eſtate
falls to a Man from a far Relation whom
he hardly ever ſaw in his Life. The E-
ſtate is much larger, and in all reſpeƈts con-
ſiderably better than that which his Father
left him, and where he was born : He
preſently reſolves, with all his Family,
to live upon it, and coming to take Poſ-
all the Country Men and Women meet
him in their beſt Cloaths; his numerous
Tennants croud about him, and though
quarrelling among themſelves, they are all
unanimous in their Shouts and Acclama-
tions to their Landlord, and every Body
thinks himſelf happy that can get but a
ſight of him. All the way he paſſes along
to his Mannor-Houſe, they Bleſs, Huzzah,
throw up their Caps, and receive him with
all the Demonſtrations of Joy that People
can poſſibly ſhew, ſaving their Wits. As
ſoon as he is ſettled. his Rents are duly
paid, and as often as he has occaſion for any
extraordinary Sums to be laid out for the
Improvement of the Eſtate. he is ſure of
Free Gifts from his Tenants, that ſhall
anſwer his Demands : Do you think ſuch a
Man that has Children and Grandchildren
whom he loves, and has ſuch a Poſſeſſion
for himſelf and his Heirs for ever, would,
after he was come to live upon it, negleƈt
and let it run to Ruin more than if his Father had left it ; or that if he underſtood
his Intereſt, he would not wiſh and promote the Welfare of theſe Tenants, as

B 2

much as thofe whom he was born among, and now for good and all come away from? If this be the King's Cafe, tho in a more glorious manner, what Prejudice can we receive from his being a Stranger?

Tant. I fay, once more every Body loves his own Country beft ; we never had a Foreign Prince to Rule over us yet, but we were always pefter'd with Swarms of the Country he came from, and I confefs I love Englifh *Men better than Strangers.*

Love. You never was fenced fo well a-gainft Foreigners as you are now ; you have an Act of Parliament, by which none but Natives can enjoy any Place of Truft or Profit, Civil or Military, throughout the Kingdom ; and then what Hurt can Strangers do us? The Strength of a King confifts in his People ; this Ifland would have been very thin of Inhabitants, if Strangers had never fettled among us. I know our Mob has ever grumbled at the coming in of Strangers, becaufe they force them to be more diligent and induftrious than otherwife they would be ; but who-ever counts that a Misfortune, is a fhort fighted Politician. Whence would you have had your Silks of fo many different Fabricks, your *Colchefter* Bays, *Norwich* Stuffs ; nay, your whole Woollen Manu-facture, which now is the Bafis of our Trade the Wealth of the Kingdom, and the fupport of the Poor, if Strangers had not brought them among you? But the Bulk of the Nation is made up of Strangers,

we

we have but few, very ancient Families among us, and the Fore-fathers of moſt of us were Foreigners once within five hundred Years. The ſucceeding Generations we ſee don't remain ſo, and let a Man come from what Country he pleaſes, he can be but a Foreigner for himſelf, all his Poſterity, if they ſtay here, muſt be *Engliſh* in ſpight of his Teeth ; I have always been, and am ſtill of Opinion, that the bringing in of Foreigners can never be counted detrimental to the Nation, at the worſt more than planting of Trees to a Family. They are chargeable at firſt, take up thatGround which might be otherwiſe employ'd and perhaps yield little or no Profit to him that plants them ; but then his Poſterity often makes Ten Pounds for every Six Pence he laid out. What muſt we have done for Ships, the Bulwark of our Nation, if our Forefathers had grudg'd to ſet Oaks ? But would you know the reaſon why the High-flyers, eſpecially the *Jacobites*, are always railing ſo much againſt Foreigners ? the *Pretender*, forſooth, was born in *England* ; they always were in hopes that the Houſe of *Hanover* being once made odious, for being Foreigners, People would turn their Eyes another way of courſe. But if we ſhould ſet aſide the many Oaths and Acts of Parliament that have been made againſt him, the little probability of his being Legitimate, and whatever elſe has render'd him incapable of ever ruling over us, what Regard could we we expe& he fhould ever have for his Native Country ; he that from his firſt Infancy was educated among Bigots, Slaves and Flatterers in a Country where Popery and Arbitrary Power ride Triumphant, and the Name of Liberty is neither heard nor underſtood ? That, as you ſaid, Men have generally a greater Affe&ion for the Place of their Birth than any other is, becauſe moſt Men are bred where they were born at leaſt till they came to ſome Knowledge, otherwiſe they love the Place of their Education far above that of their Birth; for noBody can take delight in what he remembers nothing of, and had he come among us, there is not one thing we could have hoped for from his being born here to a thouſand, we ought to have fear'd from his Education in, and his Obligations to, *France*; without mentioning what we juſtly ought to have apprehended from his Reſentment againſt the Nation for which he would never nave wanted plauſible reaſons from ſo many Reſolute Proceedings both againſt himſelf and the King, whom he believes to have been his Father.

Tant. *What do you tell me of the* Pretender, *I told you a hundred times I never was for him ?*

Love. I would not enter into your Thoughts but what elſe can the *Tories* mean, as refle&ing on all occaſions on his Majeſty's being a Foreigner, and why are they ſo fond of a Pſalm that makes mention of a ſtrange King ? His Majeſty, I

own,

own, is a Stranger by Birth, but are not the Duke of *Savoy*, and whoever you can name any ways related to the Family of the *Stuarts*, greater Strangers as well to our Country as Conſtitution both in Church and State, a thouſand times than our preſent King? What would they be at, if they are not for the *Pretender*? Would they fight againſt Providence? No Body elſe is born among us that can have the leaſt Claim to the Crown of *Great Britain*, and therefore 'tis impoſſible they ſhould have any other meaning than the Treaſonable one I ſpeak of.

Tant. *A Man may complain of a Thing as a Misfortune, and yet not pretend to know a Remedy for it, I don't love the* Papiſts, *but I am not for the* Lutherans *neither.*

Love. *Luther* began the Reformation, and his Followers were the firſt Proteſtants.

Tant. *But if King* George *had been brought up in the Doctrine of the Church of* England, *it is not probable that in his firſt Declaration he would have ſhew'd the World, that he had no greater Eſteem for it than he had for the Diſſenters.*

Love. I know what you drive at; *Epiſcopacy* and *Presbytery* are both by Law Eſtabliſh'd, the one in *England*, and the other in *Scotland*; both theſe Kingdoms are now united in one, and our preſent Sovereign the firſt Monarch that climbs the Throne with that Felicity. Now, pray tell me how a King that came with a

full

full Refolution to fecure the *Proteftant*
Religion to this united People, could exprefs himfelf more handfomely, or more
pertinently, than by afluring them, without Offence to either Nation, that he
would maintain the Churches of *England*
and *Scotland*, as they were feverally by
Law Eftablifhed? Befides, that it was
neceflary to the Peace of the Kingdom,
that mention fhould be made of the Regard theKing had for theChurch of *Scotland*,
for tho it was the Bafis of the Union that
Religion and Church Government fhould
remain unalterable in both Countries, no
fooner was the Union made, but the *Epifcopals* were encouraged in *Scotland*, contrary
to fo folemn an Agreement.

Tant. *Would you blame the Queen for pro-
moting the Religion fhe was brought up in?
Nothing is more Natural for People than to wifh
well to the Religion theyapprove of themfelves;
by this we may fee the great lofs we have fuftained
by the Death of that Pious Princefs, who was
fuch a true Nurfing Mother to the Church.*

Love. That Lofs I hope will be richly
made up in a juft and wife King, who defigns to be a Father not of one Church only,
but of two united Nations. The Union
was not forc'd upon the Queen; if a Prince
could not inConfcience have comply'd with
the Articles the Union was agreed upon,
he never ought to have fuffer'd it to com-
mence upon thofe Articles, but the Union
being once made, no King of this Ifland can
promote *Presbytery* in *South Britain*, or *Epif-*
copacy

pacy in *North Britain*, without a breach of
Truft and the utmoft Injuftice.

Tant. *Pray was it one of the Articles of the
Union that the* Scots *fhould burn our Book of
Common Prayer?*

Love. The Mob are outragious every
where when they think themfelves pro-
vok'd, but then the *Epifcopals* as well as
Presbyterians ought, where either Church
is not by Law Eftablifh'd, never to make
the leaft difturbance, and always behave
themfelves refpectfully to the National
Church, without claiming greater Privileges than what belong to the Tolleration
of their Worfhip, which if the *Epifcopal*
Clergy in *Scotland* had always obferv'd what
you complain of, would never have hap-
pen'd.

Tant. *I can't imagine why ye* Low-Church
Men are always fo over tender of the Diffenters?

Love. Do you call us over tender, becaufe we refufe to break our Contracts
with them? But you miftake your Peo-
ple, it is *Epifcopals* when you talk of *Scotland*
that diffent from your National Church,
for it is certain that even the Archbifhop
of *Canterbury* is as much a *Diffenter* at *Edinburg* as a *Quaker* or an *Independant* is in *London*; and an *Englifh* Man ought not to think
himfelf more affronted when the Common
Prayer is burnt in *Scotland*, than he would
have a *Scotch* Man when the Meeting-houfes
are burnt in *England*.

C   Tan.

Tant. But if we leave the Scots *to their own Kirk may we not promote the Church's Interest in our own Nation neither ?*

Love. By all means, who hinders you.?

Tant. May we not endeavour to bring the Schifmatiks *back to it ?*

Lov. Why don't you? Leave off Railing and Storming; and inftead of Damning and Sinking them to the pit of Hell, ufe them like Brethren, treat them like fellow Subjects, Natives of the fame Country, who by their Birthright ought to enjoy the fame Bleffings as your felves. When thus by a Friendly and winning Deportment you have difpell'd the fears and terrour you had ftruck in them before, you'll eafily perfwade them to hearken to your Doctrine: Then, 'tis your time with mildnefs and humanity to point at their Errors, and leave no Stone unturn'd to draw them from them by the moft forcible Arguments, provided that they are always as inoffenfive as they are convincing. Let the Purity and Excellence of our Church fhine forth in the Lives of its Clergy, and let it be vifible in their Beheavour as well as moft Fanatick Difcourfes, that their Zeal againft Schifm and all Errors they call Sinful, is free from human Paffion, and proceeds from a true Chriftian Spirit, which Charity is fo infeparable from. Let them preach the Gofpel, and leave State Affairs to thofe they belong to. But the Highflyers take wrong meafures to bring People over to their Sentiments, who do they think

th in

think will come to a Churc that is ever in
Danger, they frighten away whom they
should perswade. There are good and sincere
Christians among all Sects. What must an
honest peaceable Man think when he hears
some of them rail at the *Dissenters*, call their
Doctrine damnable, and their Principles vil-
lainous, and sometimes run into such fits of
Passion, that it is doubtful whether Malice
or Nonsence be more prevalent in the Dis-
course? *Men that have double rubb'd Forheads
and triple brazen Brains*; Is this an expression
a Man in his Wits would make use of? Pray
what are the mighty differences between
the Church of *England* and the *Presbyterians*?

Tant. *The more they are to blame to separate
themselves from the Church for trifles, but they
are a stubborn and obstinate People, whom
mildness and perswasion is lost upon, and nothing
but severe usage can awe.*

Love. Suppose them yet worse than you
say they are, can that excuse in our High
flying Priests the uncharitable Censures
and bitter Reproaches against them, which
Christianity condemns? What abominable
Errors can any Sect be guilty of, that wise
Men should resent with so much Wild-
ness and Violence, nay, what Crimes can
mortals commit, that ought to excite so
much Hatred and Passion in the Hearts
of an Apostolick Clergy?

Tant. *The Dissenters love to be hot themselves, but would have no body more than lukewarm that speaks against them, Would you have
no body speak up for the Church?*

Lov

Lover. I would have all fpeak up for Religion, and practife it; formerly the word Church fignify'd the People that came to to it, but our Tory Clergy mean nothing by it but themfelves, which is the reafon that moft of them are fo follicitous about the Church, and fo neglectful of true Piety and Devotion. If it was a Religious Zeal our Apoftoick Clergy has againft thofe that diffent from them, how different would both their Language and Behaviour be from what they are now? If any fet of Men had told the Apoftles, that they agreed with them in all material points of Chriftianity, but that they thought they might confefs their Faith as well fiting towards the Weft as ftanding towards the Eaft, and could have no refpect for any particular Drefs or Ceremony which our Saviour had not recommended to them, do you think they would have call'd them Fanaticks, Schifmaticks, and thunder'd out Anathemas againft them with as much Fury as our High-flyers do againft the Prefbyterians? I could yet pardon 'em, if it was the Error and not the People they are Enemies to: But not to conform to the Church is a fmall fault, diffenting from the Doctrine of Paffive Obedience, is the blackeft Crime, otherwife the moderate Church-men would not be treated with the fame inveteracy as the Diffenters are, and the moft learned and pious of the Bifhops, as well as inferior Clergy, would not be ftigmatis'd with the name of Falfe Brethren. To
read

read fome Sermons one would think there
was no other Sin than being a Whig, and
nothing was requir'd towards Salvation
befides being a Tory and to ftand up for the
High-Church. How glad are they of thofe
opportunities in which they can make their
Calumnies and Revilings feem feafonable!
What a noble handle makes a High-flyer of
the 30th of *January* to vent his Spleen and
utter the moft bitter Invectives againft the
Diffenters.

Tant. *Is not that day fet afide for a day of
Fafting and Humiliation to expiate the horrid Sin
committed in the execrable murder of the Royal
Martyr : What time can be more proper to warn
the People againft Whig Principles, that were the
occafion of it ?*

Love. The Afflictions which God fent to
Great Britain in thofe days were a punifh-
ment for the Sins of the whole Nation,
of which thofe of the King and his Minifters (unlefs you think the Court of *England* at that time to have been without)
were certainly a part.

Tant. *There you are right, lay it upon the
King, he cut off his own Head, now you talk like
a true Whig.*

Love You will never trace things from
their Origin; I'll own with you that taking
away the King's Life was a fad Difafter to
both Kingdoms, but the great misfortunes
both Nations labour'd under were not owing
to the death of the King. The mifery of the
Times confifted in the Inland Broils, the
Plunderings, and other violences committed

ted, and the reprifals continually made by
each Party, the lofs of fo many brave Men
on both fides, the general diftraction of
the two Kingdoms, and the hindrance it
was to Trade and the publick Tranquility,
with other Calamities that attend a tedi-
ous and bloody Civil War. Cuting off the
King's Head was no more than part of this
Diftraction. The common Afflictions did
not grow worfe after it than they had been
before. If we would examine into the
firft Caufes we muft look into the Grievances of the Parliament, and whether
they were redrefs'd as they ought to have
been ; Whether Favourites were not by the
Prerogative skreen'd from Juftice? When
the King had thefe unhappy differences
with his People, who was it then that advis'd him to the raifing of Ship-money and
Loan-money ? It was thefe illegal Proceedings that exafperated the Nation ; thefe
were the common Grievances, and occafion'd all the reft ; thofe that preach'd up
Paffive Obedience were more acceffary to
all the Mifchiefs than any other. Were
they the Whigs that put the King upon
thofe Arbitrary Meafures ? Did they maf-
facre the Proteftants in *Ireland* ? Did they
procure that fwarm of Jefuits about the
Court, and promote the growth of Popery
throughout *England* ?

Tant. *There is no end of redreffing what Re-*
bels call Grievances, the more indulgent he was,
the lefs they were fatis'y'd.

Love.

Love. At times the King was too indulgent, but at other times he openly violated
the Laws. The unfteddinefs and irrefolu-
tion of the Court were the effects of the
wrong meafures they took, when Parliaments had been often diffolv'd before they
could do any bufinefs, they found the
more they eluded the juftice of Parliaments, the more they rais'd the indigna-
tion of the People, and then the King
granted them they fhould fit as long as
they pleas'd. The firft was an ill ufe made
of the Prerogative, and the other was part-
ing with a confiderable branch of it; the
Conftitution fuffer'd in both. But the feveral turns of Violence and Condefcen-
dance were various Artifices which bad
Minifters made ufe of to fave themfelves,
and get the better of the People; they
were different methods to compafs the
fame ends. But thefe things have been
fet in fo clear a light, it is folly to talk of
them any more. The Ship-money alone
was enough to juftify Refiftance; the People of *England* will never fuffer any hands
in their Pockets but their own, for they
know that whoever demands a Shilling
without an Act of Parliament, may with
the fame Juftice ftrip the Nation of all
they have. To look into the firft Caufe
of the mifery that befel the two Kingdoms, you muft ask who advis'd the King
to marry a Papift; fuch a Match was likely
to do abundance of good to the Proteftant
Intereft, efpecially with a Daughter of
France

France, where it is a Saying, *That it is more the King's Interest to have* ... *Daughters* ... *in Sons because by marrying the* ... *cesses out of* ... *Kingdom they make advantageous Alliances, and are sure of Creatures in high Credit among their Neighbours.*

Tant. *You lay a mighty stress upon what one Woman could do.*

Love. What I say, the *French* are ready to own themselves: An eminent Author of that Country who wrote about 30 Years ago, counts among the presages of the future greatness of *France*, the *French* Ladies to be found in all the Courts of *Europe*; for what, *says he*, can't they bring about, having naturally a world of Charms, infinuating with great address into the deepest recesses of the Soul, esteeming it a glory to be serviceable to their Country, train'd early to the art of Intrigue, and corresponding with the Ministers of *France* at pleasure; and speaking of the Daughters of *France* themselves. he *says*, tho those Princesses are call'd Victims of State, facrifis'd against their real Inclinations, they soon forget this small violence and toil for their Country's Good. The first great Complaint of the People was the growth of Popery. of which this Match was the undoubted cause. Those that were then the King's Counsellors laid the foundation of all the Miseries that befel the Nation afterwards; those Court flatterers that endeavour'd to make the King believe that it was the King's Prerogative to dis-

penfe

penfe with the Laws of the Land ; *the* High-flying Priefts, the *Manwairings*, and others, that made Regal and Divine Commands of the fame Authority, and preach'd up Unlimited Obedience and Arbitrary Power.

Tant. I don't beleive any Church of Englan1 *Divine ever recommended Arbitrary Power to the King as a Duty.*

Love. What you'll believe I can't tell, but it is impoffible for a Divine to preach to the People that it is damnation to refift, let them fuffer what they will, but he muft at the fame time preach to the King that he may do what he pleafes.

Tant. I deny that, May not a Man, preaching to Children, tell them, that no Harfhnefs or Ill ufage of Parents can ever releafe them from the Refpeƈt and Duty they owe them ; and again, fpeaking to Parents, exhort them to Paternal Love, and inform them of the Obligations of Parents to Children ?

Love. But when this is negleƈted, and the Preachers inftead of reproving the Parents applaud the vileft of their aƈtions, and continually exhort them to ftill greater Severities ; then are not the Children in the right to think them partial, and evil Counfellors, bafe mercenary Wretches, that make a Cloak of Religion, mock God, and, unconcern d for the peace of Parents and the welfare of the Children, facrifife the felicity of both to their own Avarice and Ambition ? If Minifters, when they are to preach to Arbitrary Princes, would be fuch plain dealers as the Moderator of

E   *Edinburg*

Edinburg in his Sermon at the Coronation of King *Charles* IId of *Scotland*, I would allow them at other times to preach Paſſive Obedience to Subjects ; but a Paſſive Obedience Brieſt, when himſelf and his Party are in favour, never reproves or finds fault with the actions of his Prince, let him be Debauch'd or a Tyrant, he only ſtudies Panegyricks upon him and his Miniſters, and thunders out Anathemas againſt all that diſlike the Court meaſures.

Tant. *I don't wonder you like that Sermon, for he told the King, that they would obey him as long as he ſhould be good and rule by Law, and no longer ; and that as ſoon as he touch'd upon their Priviledges, or but offer'd to make the leaſt alteration in the Government of their Kirk, they would all reſiſt and be againſt him to a Man : He told the King likewiſe, that he had been very wicked, that God would never bleſs him unleſs he repented and led a better Life, and that the Sins of his Father and Grandfather lay heavy upon the Land, with twenty other things of the ſame ſtamp, and certainly there never was a more abuſive Diſcourſe held to a Prince's face in this World ; a Man muſt have the Impudence of the Devil to talk ſo to his King.*

Love. King *Charles* indeed had a great deal of patience at that time, and they made him Swear and Promiſe abundance of things that could not but be very diſagreeable to a Prince; they made him keep a Day of Faſt and Humiliation for the Sins of his Youth and all paſt Offences, before they would crown him, and at his Coronation they oblig'd him to ſwear, that if
ever

ever he came to the Crown of *England* he
would in that Kingdom introduce Presbytery and extirpate Epifcopacy as much as
lay in his Power.

Tant. *I believe you are forry he did not keep
his word.*

Love. I am a Member of the Church of
England, and frequent it ten to one oftner
than yourfelf, Why fhould you imagine
then that I am againft Epifcopacy ?

Tant. *Becaufe you always take part of Schifmaticks aud King-killers.*

Love. You wrong me I never did.

Tant. *Don't you fide with the Whigs, don't
you own your felf to be one, and did they not
cut off the Head of one King, and endeavour
to do the fame to his Son, if he had not narrowly
efcap'd it ?*

Love. I never juftify'd cutting off the
King's Head, yet the Difafters that befel
Kings when they begun to be Arbitrary,
are not without their ufe. and are fo many
Beacons to their Succeffors to mark out
the Sands which they are to avoid. King
Charles IId quarrel'd with his Parliament,
remov'd them up and down, and fome-
times wanted Money fadly, yet he never
attempted to raife any without the confent
of the People. His Brother *James* after
him invaded the Rights and the Liberties
of the People, but never dar'd to touch
their Pockets ; he was turn'd out for tram-
pling upon our Laws ; and you may fee
that our late Miniftry took warning by his
Mifcarriages ; their Conduct was as Arbitrary as any had been, and they would

E 2   have

have facrific'd the Nation to fave themfelves, yet were always cautious of openly
violating any Laws, contenting themfelves
with doing no more mifchief than what
could fafely be done by making an ill ufe
of the Prerogative.

Tant. *I don't know where the Prerogative
was ftretch'd in the laft Reign, if you mean making the Twelve Lords, there is nothing in it,
the Queen muft have facrific'd her Minifters
to the Fury of an Inrag'd, Difappointed and
Mercilefs Party without it ; befides, King*
William *made more Lords than the Queen.*

Love. The King has no Power or Prerogative but for the good of his Kingdom,
and there is no branch of his Authority
that was not defign'd to make him more
able to promote the Nation's Intereft than
he would be without. It is the Pr“rogative of the Crown to enoble and beftow
Titles of Honour upon thofe that for fome
eminent Services fhall deferve it; but to
make a Dozen at a time without any o-
ther reafon than to ferve a Turn, and
Skreen a bad Miniftry from Juftice, is
certainly an ill ufe made of that Prerogative : So it is likewife an undoubted Prerogative of the Crown to make Peace and
War, as the Prince fhall think fit; but to
do either vifibly againft the Intereft of the
Nation, is without all doubt an act againft
the Intent of thofe that gave the Power
to the Crown.

Tant. *Whom has the Prince his Power from,
but God?*

Love,

Love. That's another Story, the People have their Privileges, and all the Blef-fings they enjoy as much from God as the King his Prerogative; but neither are to be made ufe of but for the good of the whole : King, Lords and Commons are three parts of one Body, whilft the Con-ftitution remains they are infeparable, and fo ought to be their Intereft. But to re-turn to the troublefome Reign of King *Charles* Ift, I can't imagine why all the blame fhould be thrown upon the Presby-terians andSchifmaticks ;the difference was not between the King and the Diffenters, but between the King and his Parliament; it was the greateft part of the Nation that were apprehenfive of the danger of Popery and Slavery.

Tant. You have abundance of reafon to call that villanous Pack of Puritans that hatch'd the Troubles in Forty One a Parliament and the Nation.

Love. They were certainly the Repre-fentatives of the People, and voted, in all probability, according to their own Senti-ments, unlefs it can be made out, that the Diffenters in thofe days had aLord T —— r, or other Agent, that could fling Four or Five hundred thoufand Pounds among them, to make them vote and addrefs as he fhould bid them. The Perfecution, the Fire andFaggots in Queen*Mary*'s Days,and the many Machinations of *Romifh* Priefts to difturb the quiet of the Kingdom, inQueen *Elizabeth* s, were not forgot : They had but juft efcaped the horrid Plot, by which the

the Papifts wou'd have deftroy'd their
Sovereign, the Prince, and the greateft
part of the Nobility at one Blow. They
had fo many Inftances before their
Eyes, both at Home and Abroad, of Maf-
facres committed, and Princes murder'd by Papifts, and were fo affected
with them, when the growth of Popery
began to be manifeft throughout the Kingdom, that it is not eafy to conceive what
dread and averfion they took up againft it.
This fright, they were in, occafion'd a
thoufand extravagancies, and was likewife very Inftrumental to the encreafe of
the Diffenters.

Tant. *Which way, I befeech you ?*

Love. When Men fly from danger, it is
natural for them to run farther than they
need: The great hatred and antipathy
they had againft the Idolatry, the Superfti-
tious Rites, and other Fopperies of thePa-
pifts, made them inveterate Enemies to
all that belong'd to their worfhip, and refufe to have any thing in common with
them. As for example, the Papifts are
great Idolators of the Crofs they Carve
it, they Paint it, they Wear it, they
make Ufe of it in every part of their
Devotion, and the very make of their
Churches is to refemble the form of it :
This over fondnefs of the *Romanifts* for the
Crofs, occafion'd in abundance of Proteftants fuch an averfion againft it, that
they would not fuffer the fign of it any
where to be exprefs'd ; and fome of the
weaker fort refus'd to fee or touch it upon
a ny

any account whatever, and were as really afraid and alarm'd at it, as the Papifts would make us believe the Devil to be. It was the fame as to reading the Scripture: The Papifts were very careful in keeping the Bible from vulgar Eyes ; this was the Reafon, not only that Proteftants enjoyn d every body to perufe the Word ot God, which was commendable, but likewife which was an error, that Men of the fmalleft Capacity imagin'd themfelves qualify'd to teach others, and that every body had leave to explain the Scriptures after his own fancy.

Tant *If People were thus torn from the Church, why would the Whigs not have them re-united to it ? How can Men have the Impudence of pretending to be Church-men, and yet be againft an Act to ftop the growth of Schifm.*

Love Perfecution may rid a Country of Sects by deftroying or fending away the Sectaries, but it is the worft perfwafive in the World ; the Act of Schifm deftroys the Toleration, and ftrikes at Liberty and Property it felf.

Tant. *How will you make that out ?*

Love. Very eafily. No Property is worth a farthing without an undifturb'd enjoyment of it. If a to Man of a Thoufand a Year you fhould forbid the ufe of Salt Iron or Linnen, or any thing elfe, without which Life would be very uncomfortable to thofe that have been us'd to them, what pleafure could he have of his Eftate, and how could he think himfelf tolerated ?

Tant. *Pray does that Act hinder Diffenters from any of the Comforts of Life ?* Love.

Love. Can a Man of Sincerity, who is fully perfwaded of the truth of his Religion, and that no manner of Worfhip is fo acceptable to God as that which he embraces, ever have any comfort or enjoyment when he confiders that his Children may not be imbu'd with that Doctrine which he thinks neceffary to Salvation. What Liberty has a Man to brag of, that has not a free choice in the education of his Children? Would you not think yourfelf ftrangely injur'd if the Government, when you defign'd your Son to the Study of Divinity, fhould oblige you to make a Lawyer of him, or force you to put him out to a Wollen Draper, if yo defir'd he fhould be a Mercer? Yet this would be a lefs hardfhip than the other, by as much as the confideration of Trade is of lefs moment than that of Religion, and Temporal inferior to Eternal Happinefs. The Laws fhould be a comfort to the Juft and a check only upon the Evil-doers, but the Act of Schifm is a Law, which the worft of Men will the fooneft comply with, and no good Subject of thofe it affects can be eafy under it; for thofe that have little or no Religion will not trouble their heads about it, and laying the fault upon Neceffity fuffer their Children to be educated as you fhall pleafe to force them : But Religious and Confcientious People muft either make over their Effects, as well as they can, and leave their Native Land, or be at the charge of having their Children educated Abroad, and either

either of them muſt be a greater evil *to* the Kingdom than any can ariſe from *the* Tolleration: But you have your Act of Schiſin, would the Tories have any more, why are they not ſatisfy'd ?

Tant. *I confeſs it muſt be a great ſatisfaction for them to ſee all Places of Truſt or Profit fill'd by the Enemies of the Church.*

Love. What inconſiſtent Creatures theſe Tories are! At one time they complain that the Prerogative has been too much clipt and curtail'd by the Whigs, at another they find fault with the King's Proceedings : If the King employs his Royal Authority against the Church, ought you not to thank God and the Whigs his Power is not greater ? But pray whom do you call the Enemies of the Church?

Tant. *Theſe that undermine the Intereſt of it, and would puniſh its Miniſters when they dare ſpeak Truth in defence of it.*

Love. Pray what Intereſt do you mean, Spiritual or Temporal ? The Spiritual Intereſt of the Church is that every body ſhould reform their Lives, fear God, keep his Commandments, and love their Neighbours as themſelves, if any body declares against this Intereſt he ought to be hang'd ; and as to the Temporal Intereſt I can't ſee which way that can be undermin'd as long as the Churches, the Tythes, and other Perquiſites of the Clergy remain, and I don't hear any body is going to take them from 'em. As to the ſhare the Church has

F

in

in the Legiflative Power, there are as many Bifhops in the Houfe of Lords as there us'd to be; nor is there the leaft danger that any of thefe things fhall be alter'd.

Tant. I fhall never believe it to be the Interoft of Religion to have the Men in Power flight and difregard the Church ; a good Government ought to fupport and refpect the national Church in a peculiar manner, and not countenance every Sect that fpawns up~amongft us promifcuoufly with the Church.

Love. Which is the true Church a Man may be much better perfwaded of by himfelf than he can prove it to others that are of a contrary opinion : But the Church of *England*, as it is by Law eftablifh'd, has in every refpect as great a preheminence in this Nation over all other Sects, as Chriftians can defire. The Church of *England* Minifters have a Church in every Parifh, ready built to their hands, which is maintain'd by the Publick, whether they can conform to.it or not. The Diffenters, if they will have Meeting-Houfes , muft build and repair them themfelves, and pay to the Parifh Church befides. The Livings of our Clergy are fettl'd, and their Tythes and feveral other Perquifites are debts, which they can claim by Law ; but the Income of Diffenting Minifters is always precarious, and they have nothing to rely on but the bounty of their Congregations. None but the National Churches can have Steeples to be feen from a far, nor Bells to call the People together and fummon every body to their Worfhip. We h·ve

may

many beautiful pieces of Architecture,
lofty Cathedrals, fine Carving, Painting,
Gilding, fumptuous Organs, and Vocal
Mufick, with a variety of Dreffes and be-
coming Ceremonies, which great numbers
of People are drawn and really mov'd with,
whom Religion it felf can make but little
impreffion upon. The Diffenters are deftitute of all decorations that can pleafe
the outward Senfes, what their Teachers
can hope for from humane Affiftance lies
altogether in their own endeavours, and
they have nothing to ftrengthen their
Doctrine with (befides what they can fay
for it) but probity of Manners and exem-
plary Lives. For Students of Divinity the
Church of *England* has two famous Univerfities, where that Doctrine is ftrenuoufly
maintain'd ; they are furnifh'd with able
Profeffors, and great numbers of Learned
Men in Languages, and all ufeful Sciences, Publick Libraries, large Colleges,
Rich Endowments , and all imaginable
helps to make Men fubtle Difputants and
able Divines, with little charge of their
own ; whereas the Youth of the Diffenters,
unlefs their Relations can fend them to
ftudy beyond Sea, at a very great expence,
are forc'd to fetch their Learning at our
own Univerfities, where the Doctrine they
are to profefs is conftantly oppos d and re-
vil d, or elfe go to private Schools for it,
where, befides that they have not half the
opportunity of improving themfelves, they
are wholly at their own charge, and can
have neither Books or Inftructions but what

F 2   they

they pay for. As to Rewards and Preferments, according to which all Arts and
Sciences are promoted or neglected, the
difference is yet more confiderable. The
Difienting Minifters are almoft inevitably
condemn d to Poverty ; moft of them con-
tent themfelves with lefs than a Hundred
a Year, very few come up to Hundred
and Fifty, and none can be faid to live
in Splendour ; whereas thofe of the E-
ftablifh'd Church that will exert themfelves, have greater encouragement than in
any other Proteftant Country ; we have
many large Livings of Four and Five, and
fome of Seven and Eight Hundred a Year,
and our Clergy is allow'd a plurality of 'em.
For thofe that excel there are moreover
many Preferments in every Diocefs, befides the Bifhopricks themfelves, to fome
of which belongs (befides the Honour of
Authority) an Income of Five or Six Thoufand Pounds *per Annum*. If with all thefe
advantages over their Adverfaries our
Clergy is not able to cope with them, and
pretends ftill to be afraid of the growth of
Schifm, will not the World have reafon to
fufpect, that either the Caufe, or elfe
the Advocates, of our Church are naught ?
But it is neither Church nor Religion our
High-flyers are concern'd for ; Would you
know the ground of their heavy Complaints about the Church that it is in danger, and the Intereft of it neglected ? I'll
unfold the myftery to you. In a Nation
where the People have any fenfe of Liberty,
it is impoffible the King can trample upon
the

the Laws fafely without the affiftance of a
Clergy that preaches up Paffive Obedience
to his injur'd Subjects, who would certainly
fhew their refentments if they thought it
lawful ; this good turn deferves another,
thofe High-flying Priefts that are fo fer-
viceable to the fupport of Arbitrary Power
expect that the Prince fhould likewife pre-
fer them to what Greatnefs they are capa-
ble of receiving, and for the reft employ
no Perfons in any Office but fuch as they
fhall recommend or approve of. No Prieft
ever help'd the Prince to ride the People
but with a view of riding the Prince himfelf
afterwards, and no Clergy would ever have
fupported and efpous'd the Caufe of Tyranny and Arbitrary Power, but in ex-
pectation, that having once made themfelves neceffary to the Tyrant, they fhould
extort from him fuch Dignities, Riches
and Preferment for themfelves, Friends
and Party, as they never could have hop'd
for from their own Merit, and therefore
to recommend themfelves, and fhew what
great ufe they can be of to Princes, they
pretend to have a facred veneration for
Crown'd Heads and the Right of Inheritance, and hold it to be a damnable Sin to
oppofe the King let him be a Log or a
Crane, and do with his Subjects what he
pleafes.

Tant. *But why Pretend ?*

Love. Becaufe as foon as they are dif-
carded they alter their Note, when the
Places of Profit are not fill'd by Tories, then
Nature rebels againft Principle, then their

Clergy

Clergy is allarm'd, their *H———s* and *Sa-cheverels* breathe Hell and Treafon, while their Laity think of nothing but Plots and Aſſaſſinations. The Whigs are more gene-rous, and difown Paſſive Obedience even when they are at Helm, and have the Power in their own Hands. Is it not ſtrange the Intereſt of the Church muſt alwas be oppo-fite to that of the Nation. When the great *Marlborough* had beat all the *French* King's Generals round, our Military Glory was rais'd to the higheſt pitch, and *Great Brit-tain* was look'd upon as the Bullwark of the Proteſtant Intereſt, then the Church was in danger, and our High-flying Prieſts repin'd at every Victory as much as the *French* themſelves ; but when we had broke our word with our faithful Allies, the Na-tion's Intereſt was betray'd, our Commerce neglected and Credit loſt, then High-Church was fafe, and the fouleſt miſma-nagements were extoll'd for the wifeſt meaſures. Now again they renew their Complaints, becauſe we have a King that defigns to rule by Law, that has no Wiſhes feperate from the Welfare of his People, and our Credit is rais d again both at Home and Abroad upon the profpect of our future Happineſs. The High-flying Prieſts are the bane of our Tranquility ; when the King won't plague the People they are re-folv'd to make the People plague the King. The more the Kingdom flouriſhes the more they grumble, like Phyficians, who are never lefs ſatisfy'd than when every body elfe is well.

Tant.

Tant. *But what will you say, when the King turns out the Whigs, and takes these Tories in again that you have so much rail'd against, as he'll be forc'd to do at last? He was an Absolute Prince before, Do you think he'll ever stand under the impertinent Tutorship of Whig Parliaments?*

Love. Let the King employ whom he pleases as long as the welfare of the Nation is observ'd, I shall never trouble my head who is In or Out, and a Prince that was Just whilst he rul'd as he pleas'd, will never govern the worse when he has good Laws to guide him; but there is no fear for what you would insinuate. *Britons* are the most unfit for Slavery of any People in the World, it has been try'd so often, the least touch of a Yoak galls them, no wise Prince will ever make an attempt again upon their Liberties. A King that will be a Father of his Country, that has no Interest but his People's, that is no Slave to Favourites, but with an equal hand dispenses his Royal Favours among those that deserve them, must be a glorious Prince in *England*, and shall always command the Purses as well as Hearts and Hands of his Subjects. Let other Princes, surrounded with couching Slaves, glory in the unlimited Obedience of stupid Wretches that have no sense of Liberty, and little else to brag of, than that like so many Stocks or Stones, they can bear being kick'd and trod upon, whilst a King of *Great Britain*, almost alone in all the Universe, may boast himself to be a Monarch over Rational Creatures.

Tant.

Tant. Now I have let you run your length without contradicting you, do you imagine you have any ways convinc'd me?

Love. No, I am perſwaded Tories are not to be convinc'd, or elſe the bare reflection on their Actions would be ſufficient to ſhew them their Folly ; for how can a Man more egregiouſly contradict his Principles than by openly ſhewing himſelf a Malecontent at the ſame time he defends the Doctrine of Paſſive Obedience.

Tant. You are an incorrigible Whig, and ſo fare you well.

Love. Remember Paſſive Obedience , and then fare you well likewiſe.

F I N I S.

www.ingramcontent.com/pod-product-compliance
Lightning Source LLC
Chambersburg PA
CBHW022133280326
41933CB00007B/669